CW00517059

This

Uneven

Universe

by Benjamin Gorman

Poetry Collections by Benjamin Gorman

When She Leaves Me

Novels by Benjamin Gorman

The Sum of Our Gods

Corporate High School

The Digital Storm:
A Science Fiction Reimagining of
William Shakespeare's The Tempest

Don't Read This Book

This

Uneven

Universe

Copyright © 2021 by Benjamin Gorman

All rights reserved.

Published in the United States by
www.NotAPipePublishing.com

Trade Paperback Edition

ISBN-13: 978-1-956892-01-7

Cover Art and Design by Benjamin Gorman

For Chrystal

Thank you for all your help
putting this collection together
and inspiring a lot of it.
My world is off kilter
but you balance out so much.

Table of Contents

Uneven

Stars peeking through
thin wisps of clouds whisper
Back in the beginning
the slightest tweak of gravity
or chemical properties
could have changed things so
water molecules
would diffuse evenly
in the atmosphere,
an emulsion as immiscible as milk.
Think of it.
No clouds.
No stars.
A permanent haze.
Maybe no plants.
No animals.
No life.
So remember, say the stars
even in turbulent times
to be grateful
for the locations
of every atom
in this uneven universe

The Thrill of Altering the Course of Rivers

Tomorrow
is the day when
everything will change
good or bad but
huge, though it will
seem small at first,
tiny, like the choice
you make now which
makes it possible, so
really it's
today

About That

I am always
a little bit
embarrassed
and easily made
ashamed
so if I seem
confident
please know
I'm sorry
and I'm
embarrassed
about that
too

Thirsty Book Launch

Grovel, plead, beg them to read the words you write
Do not lose heart each time you try and fail
Writer, scream into the digital night

Every demand seems such a pathetic sight
Grasping at that elusive holy grail
Grovel, plead, beg them to read the words you write

Sinking, the sailor may loudly curse her plight
The waters which from her boat she must bail
Writer, scream into the digital night

The scolds, like abbots to the carmelite
Scornful glances demand silence till you quail
Grovel, plead, beg them to read what you write

Cry out to build your weapons in the fight
Against silent, gentle death you pound each nail
Grovel, plead, beg them to read what you write
Writer, scream into the digital night

Not Far

I can still remember
  what I was looking at
  in that moment
  on the playground
  in third grade
  asphalt
sun-bleached
and fading
  four square lines
  and a bank of
  portable classrooms
  on the horizon
  when I decided
  even if I lived
  a hundred years
  that was a very short
  amount of time and
  nothing I did
  would matter
  two hundred years
  after my death.

So, weird kid

  might be mistaken for
  a more normal
  middle-aged man

but I know
that was a very short
amount of time
ago
and my leg is still
    bounce bounce bouncing
when I sit at my desk
still in school
looking out at
asphalt
sun-bleached
and fading.

My Role

After a difficult day
the work of conversations
about who was not feeling heard
by whom
from my back porch
I listened to the big brothers
over the fence
trying to scare one another
with shouting voices
and then she appeared on the roof
of their shed
maybe five or six
and I waved.

They don't speak English
to each other and
rarely to me
but she smiled and waved back
and we shared the secret
of her impressive, forbidden
hiding place.

I wondered if she would
shout at them from there
triumphant
she deserved it and
sometimes we want to get caught.

(I would have
probably written about it
which is the same thing.)

But she snuck down
and none were wiser.
I'm grateful
for the gift of her bravery
and her smile.

Those who demand to be heard
but won't hear me
have the right to decide
who they listen to.
Sometimes it is not
my place to speak
and it is never my place
to expect to be heard.
I must learn to accept
the limits of my voice
like everyone else.
Silence is more comfortable now
since my new role model
taught me a lesson.
It can be joyous
to know
quietly.

Today And

Every day
we draft our eulogies
and attempt to sway
our eulogizers
to kindness
Every
single
day

I Had a Dream

I tried
to write it down
desperately fighting
receding fog of sleep
and burning rays of forgetting.
I don't know the characters.
Anybody, all.
She wrote a poem
about what it felt like
to be American.
They loved it.
They gave her notes
to improve it
they added four words
in indigenous languages
she could not
pronounce correctly
to be trendy
they requested more patriotism
and less but
not both
too confusing
they plugged in
slang from her culture
but not quite her slang
or her culture
they inserted
sexiness or

at least coquettishness
a little tickle, unbidden
they added four emojis
in place of
demanding vocabulary
until the feelings
didn't quite belong to her
but if she made their changes
they would publish it
they owned the channels
the promise of
maybe someday fame
maybe someday wealth
maybe someday influence
the American dream
she looked to me
for validation
affirmation these edits
were crazy, right?
wild, scared, thrilled eyes
I failed
to offer anything
but indecision
she clicked
accept changes
but couldn't recite it aloud
even if she wanted to
I never caught
her name and
her identity faded

from my flailing morning memory
but I remember their faces
the eager critics
pleasant smiles
no evil intent
not nightmare monsters
they silenced her with suggestions
praise and mild correction
just fine print
a small fee on
a stock trade
for a share of
their power
and that felt
pretty fucking American to me.

Depression Demon

Maybe mine is only
           an imp
       compared to yours
     but this is how he works.
I could make a list
    of all the activities
       which would make me happier
       and know
       they would succeed.
He sets the scrap ablaze
    with his simple incantation:
           "Why bother?
"You are unworthy of happiness."

Before

There is a space
      on the edge
         of a cliff
      overlooking the ocean
   waves and knife rocks
                              below
horizon of ocean kissing sky beyond
      toes wiggling just over
where someone could do something
unwise
   and maybe find pain
   or great, cold relief.

There is a space
         just before
          a good cry, too.
I'm not quite there.
I wiggle my toes.
My eyes ache.

Disordered

Maybe caring
  is a disorder.
Even when we
  suspect someone doesn't care
    about our concern
when we know the ones we loved
  never really cared much
    about us
when we confront the angry mob
  full of those unconcerned
    with the pain of others
we can't find
        the
        off
switch

The Darkness Begs

The photographer
frames her art
aiming at bright patches
in the night
revealing larger shapes
unseen
how startling and hopeful
the light can look
confident in its ability
to reveal more than is revealed.
I used to draw.
Copied the styles of
comic book artists
hard outside edges
desperate to identify
heroes in poses.
After decades of forgetting
I decided to try holding a brush
and placing with great care
my sweeping swaths of sadness
and droplets of tiny, pointalist pleasures
on rough canvas.
I learned
about poetry.
Don't paint the object.
Paint the light.
And my amateur
poet's paint palette

constricted and simplified
the poems drying more quickly
because the absence
is the deep void between galaxies
where the readers are gods
and swirl their worlds until
lightning strikes volcanic, fetid pools
and life grows in the cracks between.
I endeavor
to provide less
so we can see. We.
I beseech you.
Compensate for my
lack of technical skill
my failure to produce perfect realism
misplaced pixels and paint and letters and
errant words wandering
into darkness
so we can
create together

Porcelain

Do you know why
toilet bowls
are so smooth?
Imagine the grime
that would
build up
in the cracks.
I have never been smooth.
I used to be optimistic, though.
I have experienced
a lot of
growth

Carcinogenic

Has anyone come across
　　　　good research
on a causal relationship
　　　between
cancer of the guts
　　　and
　　holding your tongue?

Unwise

Every time someone
tries to tell me
        "You shouldn't write about that"
they pour a little
        tiny

          p
          i
          s
          s
          y

          t
          r
          i
          c
          k
          l
          e

        of fuel
      on a smoldering match
      while holding the gas can

Flailing

thought I'd write a poem
capturing this feeling
in my shaking fists
and throwing it out to the world
to let it go
but it was just one four letter word
repeated
repeated
strung down the page
line after line
like the chain on a
medieval flail
ending in a metal ball
of larger letters and
exclamation spikes
and those weapons
must be wielded with great care
because they swing back

Falling into Hard Holidays

When I was a child
premature nostalgia
imbued the everyday
with the prophecy of a life
reflected upon fondly
while holding a magic stone
the colors of falling leaves
or a ray of sunshine
which chose an unusual angle
to illuminate dust motes
shaped in the letters
of the lost language
of magic spells.
Or, when I was a young man
holding a warm hand
in crisp fall air,
a promise of
warmth in our winter. But
now my sentimentality
works normally
a mirror on the objects
that conjured nothing
portents of a tale I was telling
myself alone which
would not come true.
I foresee the last season
will be ice and silence.

Gratitude in 2020

The liquid soap
on the dishes
is just green goo until
churned, it becomes bubbles
and people keep popping up
on my phone
excited by isolation.
Vicky, the poet, talks about
sharing and gives me a prompt
and Eleanor, the writer, says,
"I'm not bailing on what I've got, but just
whew … I've reached for
someone else's dream, it feels like"
and Jessica, a tired new mom,
tells me about her son's meltdown but
she pluralizes to
"We are tired and want to be held"

That's the year.
When the country discovered its
deeper rot in the middle
of a plague and only barely
tossed out the dictator after
so much damage
and so many standing
with signs that really said
"We are tired and want to be held"

and Thanksgiving could be
obligatory and false except
I'm grateful
for all the bubbles

Reconsideration

I am not
a religious man
    but when I was a child
   when I spoke as a child
  when I understood as a child
when I thought as a child
   I judged Zeus
 the villain of the story.

But now
   as I watch men
     beat one another
  to death with
 bloody flag poles
    and lands
     with names that ring
   of Greek mythology
   Australia, California,
  the home of the Amazon,
 burning,
conflagrations the size
      of empires,
I reconsider.

Whatever deity
    who,
   out of titanic love
shaped this race from mud

and who,
out of infinite naivete
gave such beasts
the paired gifts
of speech
and fire
deserves to have
his liver ripped out
each day
by vultures.

Celebrate

Exhausted talking heads announced
the dictator of mulch and cremation
would keep fighting fruit
-lessly, but he's
finished, finally, flamed out
of office and that's when
she reached over the transom
where I look the best
dressed in words. She was scared
to leave the house in this
America where "economic anxiety"
makes her skin a target,
but she didn't mind
the skin that has kept me safe
for all these years.
She didn't want to talk politics
or anything else really, just
celebrate, so she couldn't learn how
these years have bruised me
and wouldn't have
cared. I presume it's been worse
for her wearing her perfectly smooth
unsafe skin with the feather
tattoo hidden on her back
which shuddered when kissed.
Her smile irradiated my bones
and she bit me hard enough
to remind me to allow myself to

feel relief. I don't know
if there will be a mark
but she left an impression
that we may celebrate again someday
and this is how to build a better life
sharing time and sharing space
in unfettered joy

Veil

My modern mourning
clothes, course sackcloth
take the form
of microns of soft dust
on picture frames.

The kind that hold
multiple photographs
have some images removed
but the dust
remains
strategically settled
like snow on sills
top and top
above and beneath
the empty spaces.

And I know the mourning
veil is lifted
as I wipe away the past
to place new pictures.

Mirror Distortion

A black hole
  consumes everything.
    Even light
      falls inside,
      matter
        is s t r e t c h e d
      until it crosses time
          and is broken
                 forever
      but still falling

She refuses to recognize herself when she
  looks in the mirror.
  the self-recognition test
  applied to animals
  has been stolen from her by
  humans who have told her
    that what she sees is not
               her

I can stand behind her
  and see her
    strong arms
      soft skin
        mother's breasts
        lover's smile
  generous eyes

always generous
to a fault
  giving every kind of
    compassion
      and secret
      neutron-heavy self-consciousness
      and depleted-uranium shame

                And just maybe
                      maybe
                      maybe
                that is my self-recognition test
                a dollop of ink
                  generous,
                    lovingly
                      placed on my forehead
                by her eyes
  becomes my black hole
    and time s t r e t c h e s
  the rate of my movement
  matching her brokenness
  seeing her as she is
  she sees me as I am
distorted to ourselves
and we fall
and fall
and
fall

Imbeautiful

Perhaps
our natural inclination
to admire symmetry in nature
                faces with eyes of the same size
                flowers without missing petals
                        even teeth
                        smiles over sneers
                        four legged dogs and
                        two-winged birds
is less about efficiency
                        two wings for flight
                        four legs for running
                        smiles for welcoming
                        teeth for chewing
                        petals for attracting bees
                        eyes equally opened
                        but equally skeptical
more about the knowledge
                        that so much pain
                        comes from one side
                                loving more
                                the other
                                        less

Too

I have been here before
open eyes
white wall staring
closed mouth
teeth pulverizing one another because
they have no way to
escape this either
heart doesn't know whether to
beat fast or beat slow or beat at all
every breath just a little
too shallow too little
future too little hope
to fill two lungs

Self Care

Before takeoff
they always remind us
to put the masks on ourselves
first.
Fine but
I bet
when the engines fail
and the nose points down
they forget
to come on the mic
to shout over the screaming
a reminder
to put the masks on others.

The angle
of the world feels
off to me.
My little window is filled
with flames.
What made the fans
tire of twirling?
What made the gears
abhor one another's teeth?
I suspect
it's the weight
of the wrong reminder.

Backwards

Imagine if wars were fought

                                    backwards.

All the death and pain
would slowly be
remembered
until finally a small group of soldiers
filthy and bloody and exhausted
would march

                                    backwards

into a field of bodies
aim their rifles
and suck the bullets
out of the corpses of their enemies
bringing them back to life.

Then these large groups of excited youth,
clean and healthy,
would return

                                    backwards

to their families
who would forget their new worries.

And the profiteers
who made the life-giving rifles
would undiscover their excuses
to send so many to that newly cleaned field.
And the profiteers would give money

                                                    backwards
    to those
    newly happy families
    to raise those children.

          What a glorious, stupid world that would be.

    It makes you think,
    we could choose to go
forwards
    to ignore the profiteers' excuses,
    keep the money for our children,
    forget the hatreds
before
    they cause the death,
    and we could make a world
    almost as amazing as that one
    and even less stupid and less

                                                    backwards

    than ours.

Controlled Temperature

A mild summer
  all things being
            relatives are far away
       lovers moreso
  beds cold
sweatier online than off
      humid inside
          masks and fogged glasses
        and quarantine quarters
      air still spicy from
  lingering wisps of teargas
and heated by
  the hot breath of
    frightened white denial
      that shouts so loud
         with so few words
  and the flames of
      righteous Black rage
        that waits so long
         to burn so brightly
  and the thousands of tiny
          pathetic, flickering
      hopeful stars of
    another candlelight vigil
  and another candlelight vigil
  and another candlelight vigil

Learning to Speak

We learn so young
        to say
        I'm sorry
then later
  that we should forgive
        forgiveness
  takes more work but
in the meantime we say
        I'm sorry
        for more and more and more
  until we find a way
      to apologize away
              and away and away
    and I still haven't learned to say
apology not accepted.

Forgotten

The virus
  does not care
   that you are tired
   of wearing a mask.
The virus
  does not care
   that you've mostly been careful
    and are just making an exception
    for a special occasion.
The virus
  does not care
   that vaccination rates
   are going up.
The virus
  does not care
   about almost there.
The virus
  does not care
   what you read on twitter
   or heard from your uncle's
    ex-wife's former son-in-law who
   may be a doctor of
   something.
The virus
  does not care
   who you voted for
   or who your mask will upset.
The virus

does not care
 about your concern
 that the vaccine
  was produced quickly
  or who will profit from it
   or which countries will get enough.
The virus says,
 "I don't like politics," and
 "Both sides," and
  "Sure, but what about..."
  (Both sides are
  nostrils
 and what about is
 your throat because)
The virus
 only cares
 about finding
  a welcoming foyer
  in your nose
  and a roaring hearth
   in the living room
   of your lungs
   where it can keep
   its children warm
    and when they are ready
    to leave the nest
     send them out to find
      happy homes of their own.
The virus
 does not care

about your opinion.
"Keep sharing it,"
says the virus.
"Loudly, please."
"There were millions
and millions and millions
who can't disagree now
because they have been
silenced.
"I'm so glad
you've forgotten."

Open Question

I do wonder
 whether your ethos
  is "owning the libs"
  or "all government action is bad"
  or "profit over people"
  or "caring about others is socialism"
  or just "masks are inconvenient for

                                    me"
                                   "me"
                                   "me"

when one million Americans are dead
         one million Americans
 will you choose to fail
  to see the connection

or worse
 will you call it
a victory?

My grandfather is going to die today

My country is sliding away, too
 in the morphine haze
 a cartoon villain is king
 people are shouting in the streets
 because they are so afraid
 to admit they are so afraid

My house is a yawning well
 I climb out of and put on a mask and
 pretend to be brave but
 I shout that I am afraid
 with a desperate sign
 and I try to hold onto hope
 with nothing but pictures of flowers
 and I fail a little more
 with every
 falling petal

The newspapers print
 a running count

My grandfather is going to die today

Classroom

Look at their faces.
Memorize them.
The girl there
 with the brightest smile
  is living her slave ancestor's dream.
She can go to college
 buy a house
  choose when to have her own children
   own her own beautiful skin.

And that boy there
 was called a girl
  but he can get the body he wants
   and be loved by the person he wants
 and learn to love himself.

And look at her
 the girl whose parents took a boat
  to escape a war
 and a plane to escape an unwelcoming land
and bus ride to escape an unwelcoming city
 and made a home
   where she is welcome.

And that boy
 who is learning English
  so he can translate at the doctor's office

and tell his mother
　that he will someday
be the doctor
　who can translate
　　for another mother.

And look at that boy
　who hates them all
　　because their futures are brighter than their ancestors'.
He hates them
　because he will not have a plantation
　　or women to rape at will
　　and he sees this as a loss
　　　that they must pay for
　to make America great again.

And we make damned sure
　he has the right
　to his opinion
　　and to the gun in his hands.

Marching

White man
running late for the
Black Lives Matter march
401 years too late
desperately
scanning the car for sunscreen
wouldn't want to
hurt for this
wouldn't want to
burn

I pass
lines of men and women
picking fruit in the fields
how many not offered
humanity because
papers please?
How many could have
children thrown in
cages in concentration camps?
while they
burn
to feed families
theirs and mine?
Ours?

Where is my sunscreen, anyway?

They march
    up and down the rows
      their backs bent
       worthy of more respect
         demanding more recognition
          of their dignity
           and humanity
    than my calendar entry
afternoon stroll for justice.

          My event
        was postponed after all.
      Something about permits
    not processed in time by
white bureaucrats.
Guess I missed the memo.
401 years too late
        I walked through the city
        with my sign
      nodded at other white people.
    All pleasant. No objections.
                  No one
                      burned.
      We all smiled
      behind masks
    knowing the fruit would be
    cheap.

White God

I'm beginning to understand
why white America
so desperately needs an old
bearded, white God

If white America
could fathom
a Black God
who is infinitely just
we might also see
there will be no white Americans
in His heaven

The Beauty of Damage

At so many protests
America damaged her vocal cords
shouted herself hoarse
and then sang
more honestly than ever

The echo of the shouts
scraped the drums
of America's ears and made them
sensitive to truths she had not heard

Stores were looted
restaurants burned
maybe the start of
America's healthier new diet

Books were cracked open
their perfect spines sacrificed by
an America seeking to understand
her roles and responsibilities
in causing and healing
so much damage

and which damage is ugly
and which damage is beautiful

Blood Eagle

The most severe punishment
a Viking could inflict
on an enemy he hated
and respected
was to make him
a blood eagle.
The enemy was bound
arms outstretched
and the torturer
would cut open his back
break his ribs
pry open the cage
pull out his lungs
and drape them over
his shoulders
like scarlet dripping wings
and through it all
if the victim could remain conscious
and not cry out
he could still earn his place
in Valhalla.

On the day
of the dawn of
the new year
I will stand on one side
of the street and shout
at the chud the proud

boy the patriot
prayer.

We will demand
surrender. We won't
get it.

But first
let me bind myself
arms outstretched
teeth clenched and
refusing to pass out
because if I can love him
that is empathy, my paradise
of pointless, unceasing battle
to prepare myself for
the Ragnarok of my own
enlightenment, which I know
I will lose.

We share so much
he and I, it
should be easier.
He will stand, back rigid
jaw set, his body
placed between
his America and
the enemies who want to
make it something else.

That alone is worthy
of respect.

But we have more.

He believes in false stories
with as much passion

                       as the cosplayers and fanboys
                       and blerds I love so much. We
                       have our marvelous heroes and
                       treks through the stars
                       shipping Scoobies and Whovians
and he dresses up and rolls
for initiative to battle through his
dungeons of hippies and
dragons of Jews running
child sex rings in pizza parlors.

                       I can hate his story but love
                       his nerd-dom, his commitment
                       to fantasy. I write novels
                       teach literature, invented stories
                       heat my house and
                       juice the microwave
                       that excites the molecules of
                       my dinners. I live on fiction
                       and can love him for that.

He would never
pour gallons of
water into the tank
of his truck. He knows the
limits of his fiction. He chooses it
not because it's false but
because it works
just like every
religion ever invented

and when it doesn't he
fights the pagans to
hold onto truth and justice
and freedom

        truth and justice
        and freedom

                truth and justice
                and freedom and every
                good thing. I can love
                that while also
                seeing the bodies
                sacrificed to the
                profits of the priesthood
                the crusade to hold onto
                the holy lands, their
                soil made fertile by
                the blood of the
                children of infidels
                gentiles, heathens,
                gaijin, illegals,
                foreigners, savages,
                barbarians, liberals,
                communists, apostates.

He was told
his pale flesh
and penis that pointed
him the right way
would earn him respect
but all they gave him
were the advantages he
can't see from inside

and love he cannot feel.
He won't want my empathy
but he needs the honor
of those other men beside him
to feed his hunger for glory

                    and I am so parched
               for fountains of human contact
                         I can love that.

His torture
has lingered far longer
than Viking punishment
a whole lifetime of
cutting to expose
his heart to the cold
so it cannot beat for
anyone but the white men
on his side of the street
and the flags they love once
they've changed the colors
and the leader who is
a hollow idol but
in his emptiness
the paragon of their
disdain as virtue.

               On New Year's Day
             we'll put on our armor
              bring our best weapons
his gun, his sympathetic
local police (professional maintainers of

the status quo), his
bigger fists, his
history

my bullhorn, my vigilant
streamers (amateur
citizen journalist witnesses), my
bigger words, my
future

We'll both think ourselves
better armed
We'll want the other to see it our way
but expect little
and get less.

Hating me
a libtard Jew race-traitor
helps him
make sense of his world
so he's already won
without trying.

Loving him
a white-supremacist fascist
would help me
make sense of mine
but I've tried now and
already failed.

He gets his Valhalla.

I cry out.

Inauguration Day, 2021

Democracy must be reborn
again and again
and we met on the day
of the near-miscarriage
close thing
245 years is a lot of trimesters
taken for granted, and
late-stage the placenta of truth
necessary to carry us all
was almost separated
from the uterine wall of our institutions
still touch-and-go, frankly, but

This morning we held each other
while listening to the
crackle of the alarm radio
clicking back through time
to families comforted by FDR.
The words were shaped
like the vault of a cathedral
the delivery
a warm casserole
in the low-ceilinged basement potluck.
That's his greatest gift
to speak the coldest truth
and make it sound like
"Welcome"

We the People
in one another's arms
squeezed in gratitude
at the sound
of certain unexpected
but longed-for phrases
We the People
pulled into one another
shared breath of
shared hopes
We the People
felt a little taller
a little lighter
We the People
floated a little higher
rising up out of
years of winter.

Democracy is crowning
born again for another day.

Half

At this midpoint
I suspect
half of wisdom is
discerning what should be released
and the other half
what should be retained.

I grasp for every
lover who is gone
or was never there
every time I misspoke
or missilenced
every word that made me sneer
or broke my heart again
so much abject stupidity
cruelty masquerading as ignorance
and ignorance donned as armor
my fury at humanity

I hold onto too much
half a fool

but as I sink
into the end of the latter half
my memory will release
every lover who stayed
and stayed

every kindness I offered
and received
every arrangement of letters which
filled my rib cage with too much
admiration leaving no room for air
dizzy with joy of language
and love of humanity
every discovered bloom
and wide-eyed infant's
surprised glee
will be released as well

I will hold nothing
half a fool

Stutter Step

There are things I should be
feeling now
and I am but
not about the right things
it's like
that tweet about a
historic moment
every six seconds
those events
should have me terrified
and I am but
my terror comes from
hope

That day
they stormed the capitol
high treason on every
glowing screen
that should have
been so many things
the end of their movement
the end of the demagogue
the end of a winter of years
but the blizzard drags on
and I should be terrified
and I am but

I am because
the beautiful woman
wearing guillotine earrings
said "I put something
special in the bag
for you"
and the note on the dessert
said "Because I'm antifa
and I can!"
And I am because
that just may
have changed my life
more than
anything

Letting It In

The voice
    on the TED Talk
says the biggest impediment
    to love is shame
and shame is feeling unworthy of love.

        Shame is a stone rolled in front of the tomb
                and there is no Easter.

and I know why she keeps making me
    repeat, "I am worthy."
but I also know tomorrow
    she may say, "So sorry, but
I never really loved you.
    I was just pretending.
I didn't realize that until now."

It's happened before.
    I feel unworthy
because I was found unworthy

        Push the love away
      and there will be no hole
         when it turns out
          it was never there.

and the voice on the TED Talk

says vulnerability is the cure
so I pull over
    and cry
and admit it.

Mirror

Sometimes I
     stop
and feel guilty.
  I must be taking advantage.
  How selfish.

        I love her
because I love the way
    she loves me
when I'm just being
    me.

How broken
 would a person have to be
 to love me that way
  when I'm not even pretending
 to be
   someone else?

     Then I see
  how broken I am.

She loves me
 because she loves the way
 I love her
  when she's just being
   her.

Folded Space

The dog is downstairs
with the boy and
you are in your own bed
                      across town.
In the chrysalis of blankets
punctured by a wrinkle
blowing a frigid
breeze on three toes
but the insomnia
is a virus spread by
the silence which starts to seethe
pulses out pounds of pressure
too much atmosphere
pressing on eardrums
like hunger pulling a stomach
                    towards a spine
without your gentle murmurs
and hums and occasional
chuckles at the dog's snoring
I hear absence ringing so loudly
the distant whines and yips
of the pack of coyotes
are comforts

When

When someone discards you
and breaks your heart
don't try to glue it
or squeeze it
or force it back into shape.

Let it remain.

When you find yourself
filled with happiness again
it will be brighter
as the light
shines through the cracks.

Kleptothermy

She taught me
 a new word.
Kleptotherm.
It defines
 too much
  about my everyday neediness
  and all those who came before
growing resentful
going cold
 but it also illuminates
  why she and I
 feed off one another
and burn
so brightly.
I dare not
 forget.
We are shared
 heat and light.

Lesson Sea

When you learn it
   not just flirt with the idea
  but feel it wrap around your
bones and squeeze
the revelation, the notion
the possible truism
  that all feelings are choices
    including love
you may have to flounder and flail
to stay above the flood of feelings
    the regret of loves poorly chosen
    the anger at loves
      who did not choose to love back
    the joy at all the possible loves
     you could choose tomorrow
    today
   right now
  the fear of choosing poorly again
and then you may land on the beach
 gasping and coughing up the past
 salt and sand and tears and bile
  vomited spluttering shock
because even this wave
 is also a choice
 and it recedes
  in quiet contemplation
   of loves more carefully considered.

The Heavy Words

I fear
the love
we share
is so mixed
with the fear
we learned
at the hands
of others
swirled
the purest holy water
the venom of a monstrous fang
clouding together in a chalice
to the sound of an incantation
whispers of affection
curses spat at our pasts
to call forth
a demon of doubt
who makes the firmament
a crisp page of thin ice
where we dare not place
the heavy words.
We hold on
with our hands
our arms
our teeth
our lips
could betray us
if either misspoke

and sounded too much
like those
who left
before.
We must learn
to shape the words
within that embrace
to hold
the fear
inside
the love
if we'll ever hope
to hear
what we listen for.

But you go first.

Something She Said

She said something
   not that something
a different something
  but also something
I've heard others say
         before

but when she said this something
  the something they'd also said
   I knew she meant it
    she showed she meant it
  and it made me suspect
I'd never really heard this something
     from someone
      who meant it
        before

Most Romantic Date

She didn't balk
  at my suggestion
for an activity
  for date night
a nap
  on the couch
    after many long days
                apart
            drifting off
  her head on my chest
became the sunlight
  blanketing a field
the room's still air stirred into
     a spring wind over
    carefully painted
      dew drops
      on lips
I asked her to
remind me
to write the poem
of the warmth
of her body
of the cool
of the kiss
when we awoke
comfortable
comforted
comforting

You

When the ship capsizes
And the water is too cold and too much
And fills my lungs
I will try
To be buoyant enough
That you can hold onto my corpse
And survive

When the ground shakes
And yanks out the foundation
Pulling every beam askew
And the ceiling surrenders to its weight
And proves my skull's fragility
I will try
To land sideways
So you can wedge yourself
In the width of my shoulders
And survive

When the brakes go out
On the city bus
And the wide white crosswalk lines
Offer no protection
I may let go of your hand briefly
And my slow wit
That can never invent the punchline in time
Will fail to alert my limbs
Thus discovering the last joke but

I will try
To be soft
And absorb
So you can rebound
And survive

When the blizzard
Of all the little cold, furious, buzzing
Distractions I employ to hide
From myself
Melt away
And my need to be the hero
And the center of the storm
Resolves into a man-shaped
Soggy pile of drowned, buried, flattened, unread books
No hero, not much of a poet, sometimes barely a person,
not much, but
I will try
To say, "I love you
"I believe in you
"I do this for you
"For you
"You."
And I will try
To lift you
To hurt with you
To hold you
So you can smile
And survive

Clear Sky

Cloudless
and the sun beamed
a sky of crystalline joy
the day her mother died
and she knew herself
and knew her mother
and knew her mother and herself
well enough
to feel guilty
for feeling guilty
for not feeling sad.

New Fish

I remember the moment
in her story when
she becomes one with the ship
and she sees the universe
through the skin of the fish
who floats them all between worlds
only momentary confusion
discombobulated but not terrified
when she transcends her body
but does not lose her self in the void
and then she is one with the fish
breathing in what it gives her
safe inside but daring outside
to flip and spin and
more courageously
know the vast emptiness
she can fill with her second chance at life
weightless or grounded on some distant world
as she chooses

Rememberers

Movie ticket stubs
   make the best bookmarks.
They remind about a story
   and remember a place in a story
  and stories are all that's worth
  remembering when all you want to do
is forget

Hair

The individual strands
of my beard
can't decide
if they want to be
Jewish curly or
Scottish wavy or
Irish thin or
Portugese thick
but they're finding
consensus on
old-man gray and
untamable wiry
that's fine when
she falls asleep
on my shoulder with
strands of her long, straight, bright purple hair
and mine hold on
Velcro gripping
which feels
fitting

For Van Holstad

When an emptiness
appears suddenly
the universe pushes and pulls
nature becomes abhorrent
and when the vacuum is large
a panther closing glowing eyes
in the darkest night
this new void
shaped once like a pillar
of strength and caring
and all the goodness we
looked to as our sense of
our collective self
the sheer size of the space
which must be filled
pulls us off our feet
rips the air
rent like the curtain
in the Temple
and as we fall inwards
we must reach out
desperate fingers and
shouted names
dodging detritus
grab onto one another
hold on as we tumble
into the new fire
of his memory

Nothing Supernatural

As keychains go
it was absurd
so large it rubbed holes
in the pockets
of Amber's jeans and
caught on everything and
weighed so much she
always dropped her keys but
her uncle told her it was
lucky
she was seven when
he gave it to her with
a story
about fairies
or sprites
or gremlins
it wasn't clear
if he knew the difference
some small
winged creature
trapped inside
a hunk of metal
roughly a disk but not
flat enough to be a coin
bulging in the middle where
the creature
was trapped in the circle

of the runes carved in it
carved so deeply
they made holes around the edges
holes big enough to
bend a keyring through
and hang her housekey
and the fob for her Toyota
isn't fob
a ridiculous word?
almost
as ridiculous
as believing some creature
was captured
entombed alive
buzzing and angry and
spitting magic
like a Fourth of July sparkler?
who would want that
in their pocket?
but she was seven
a magic age
and now Amber was 23
and missed her uncle and
not so unmagical
that she'd throw it away
but old enough
to be embarrassed when
she pulled it out of her pocket
in a parking lot
as a couple passed by
and the woman with bangs glanced

at the flash that might have been a knife
and started
and the man with
a mustard stain on his shirt glanced
at his wife and
chuckled at her fear because
men get to do that
and the woman
shared a telepathic moment of understanding
with Amber because
women get to do that
but the moment was cut short when
Amber dropped her keys
again
because the chunk of metal was
so heavy
and also maybe the keychain
jumped a little
or buzzed
or shocked her but
certainly that couldn't be
possible
even less likely
than the crow that flew right over her back
there were crows in the parking lot
no big deal that it swooped
between the cars and through the space
right where her
face would have been
and it didn't harm anyone

didn't even hit the
easily startled woman with bangs
who screamed and fell backwards
into the man with the mustard stain
who laughed again
and stepped back
into the path of the car
that was only going
a little bit fast for
a parking lot
and it really wasn't the driver's fault
she didn't have auto insurance because
neither of her jobs paid enough
for rent and food and gas and insurance
and it really wasn't the mustard stain man's fault
he didn't have health insurance
because his company cut his hours
and it wasn't the company's fault because
they just wanted to compete with
a company somewhere else which
also didn't offer health insurance
or enough to pay
for rent and food and gas
and auto insurance
but the driver would lose her
apartment and live
in the car she could no longer drive
there's nothing supernatural
about being trapped inside
a hunk of metal
and the mustard stain man would lose his

house because of the
medical bills the driver couldn't pay
and his wife with the bangs would lose her
fear of muggers when she had no money
but she wouldn't lose her fear of parking lots because
women don't get to do that
and the mustard stain man's
company would lose to
that company somewhere else but
the owners would still have health insurance
and Amber would only gain
a disquieting story to tell
the guy behind the counter
at the Toyota dealership
when she went to get a replacement
for the broken fob
and felt embarrassed when
the guy saw her keychain and
raised an eyebrow
so Amber sealed herself
in the protection of a story
just a story
nothing supernatural about those
just that some people are lucky
lucky
enough to drop a keychain and
reach for it
to hold onto
magic

Patient Velocity

A passionate velocity
joins some people
together but
is there a
patient velocity?
A potential of speed
where rotors spin up
and electricity heats
copper coils until they
crackle and blaze
while the entire apparatus
sits,
just
sits,
waiting to collide
with the life of a person
who is also idling
unknown
just
around
the corner?

Perfect Seventy-Seven Degrees of Rotation

Crafting an intricate, dense, complex,
polyglot, metaphysical, demanding
poem but
         taking a break to
write a poem
           about writing a
  poem but really
   mostly sitting
 in the sun on
a Saturday
and listening to
   a neighbor's saw
   another's lawnmower
   and neighbor birds
    singing about territory
     seed discoveries
    budding romances
while my dog
  pants a smile
    scratches her back
  with the warm grass
I am
swaddled in poems.

Polvo

This rite
is an attempt
to pluck the right
one when I write
but even when correct
they sound
off.

Though инстина (pravda),
they are not правда (istina).

In the beginning
I've been told
there was the λέξη (léxi).
This μύθος (mýthos) appeals
to a lover of words.

But when my world
is barren, bereft of the moisture
of both syllables and significance
I have a *sueño* of a desert of *polvo*
polvo
velvet between fingertips
slipping through
the spaces in unmartyred hands
such a softer word
than "dust"

And a swirling globe of *polvo*
might become *la tierra*

so much more majestic
than the choked ululation
the sorrow-less sob
of "Earth"

My bitterness
at this sound
this world named
after something like dough
dropped accidentally on
something like ground
my resentment
is a feeling unlike
the birdsong flute of *ceniza*
more the viper-strike of "ash"

There is a gas
which fills the space between
polvo and dust
between *la tierra* and the Earth
between ash and *ceniza*
it's just a ghost, mayhap
a נֶפֶשׁ (néfesh)
a ψυχή (psychí)

The gap between languages
whispers in the darkness
Don't look at my face
and I'll tell you a secret.

Even in the beginning
even before the beginning

there was no "truth"
it confides.
Truth came later
plosive and astounded
then slinking away
"truth"
nor was there the verdad
you crave
sidling up with a joyous smile
to bump you with a generous hip
and a laugh
verdad

No, there were only
hungry, yawning mouths
wanting words
for meat and knives
to carve the flesh
and armor to defend
against the blades
sword and shield and meal
of purpose and meaning
but you are naked
and disarmed
and starving because
you are dust
hoping desperately
to become more than dust
but you will never be
as beautiful as
polvo

Somehow

In spring
the flowers
on the pear tree
appear too fast
for me to notice each one

Somehow

this helps me
make peace
with all the books
I will never get to read

Strange Confession

I know it sounds odd
but I still sleep best
when my son
is in the same room.
It happens very rarely now
when we are in a tent
or crashing at a friend's
while on vacation
and it will happen less and less
and then not at all
until he sleeps in a chair
while I'm in a hospital bed.

It takes me right back
to his infancy
when the proximity
meant knowing
he was breathing.
My happiest time.

And when I am in that paper gown
And he's a grown man
maybe even an old man
rumpled and disheveled
positioned uncomfortably in the chair
maybe snoring like his old man
I will drift off for the last time
knowing he is breathing
and I'll
rest easy.

Agnostic Worship Service

The grass will grow back.
The weeds will return.
The cursed blackberries will recover.
And yet
  a day spent in the garden
    never feels
      wasted.

Why?
             This is a holy
    inexplicable mystery.

My end
  is even more inevitable
             than the yard's entropy.
I hope
  in years to come
    to learn to believe
      my life has been
        a good day's work.

Employment Preview

Your last job
will be to lie down
in a hole
or in a vase
or blow in the wind
and then be less and less
while you are less and less
remembered.
Lest you get depressed
consider:
You will be 100% perfect
at this task.

In your performance evaluation
no middle manager can conceive
of a better way to do the job
than you will do.

No matter how you struggle
at living,
slow down.
Take your time.
You are moving
inexorably
toward being
perfect
at not being.

A Poet Splashing

We tell the story
to warn ourselves
not to fly too high
but we don't tell the story
of those who watched Icarus fall
but wouldn't dare to leap

Just One

A solitary
accomplishment
in an entire day
can seem paltry
just one victory
in so many hours
but do the math
a life of such
compounded
would be a triumph

Just a Poet

So maybe
I'm just a poet now.
And maybe someday
being just a poet
will be enough
for somebody.

About the Author

Benjamin Gorman is an award-winning high school English teacher, political activist, author, poet, and co-publisher at Not a Pipe Publishing. He lives in Independence, Oregon with bibliophile and guillotine aficionado Chrystal, his favorite son, Noah, and his  dog, E.V. (External Validation). His novels are *The Sum of Our Gods*, *Corporate High School*, *The Digital Storm: A Science Fiction Reimagining of William Shakespeare's The Tempest*, and *Don't Read This Book*. His first book of poetry, *When She Leaves Me*, was published in November of 2020. He believes in his students and the future they'll create if given the chance.

Also Available from Not a Pipe Publishing

Brief Black Candles
by
Lydia K. Valentine

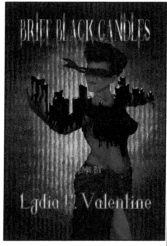

"In *Brief Black Candles,* Lydia Valentine attends, with passionate velocity, to questions of survivability, remembrance and the creative art of living a fully human life, even in contexts and conditions that work against that what-it-could-be. ...reading becomes a mode of witness. ... Haptic, revolutionary and unflinching, this is a powerful debut collection by a poet who does not, and cannot, 'in this time-/ in this place-', look away."
  -Bhanu Kapil

"This debut collection, written in the most truthful key available to language, uses poetic form and precise repetition to give shape, then echo, to questions of family, loss, justice and survival, seated in the frame of an America that is a long way from post-racial—the America of today."
  -Sanam Sheriff

Wherever Fine Books Are Sold

Also Available from Not a Pipe Publishing

When We Talk of Stolen Sisters
by
Jessica Mehta

WHEN WE TALK OF STOLEN SISTERS

NEW AND REVISED POEMS BY
JESSICA MEHTA
AUTHOR OF *SAVAGERY* AND *THE WRONG KIND OF INDIAN*

This collection of Jessica Mehta's powerful, beautiful, vulnerable work spans "from dates so long ago I can't even recall" to her most current poetry in the midst of a pandemic. Her poems call our attention to the unsung disappearance of Indigenous women, the cultural genocide that still continues, the eating disorders that consume us from within, and to love, family, and the courageous choice to see the world from a different angle in the face of death.

"... book smarts *and* street smarts, and that combination makes this collection completely *uncontainable* ... Mehta overflows with life, and we **are** lucky that the spillage produced these poems."
  -Linzi Garcia, author of *Thank You*

Wherever Fine Books Are Sold

Also Available from Not a Pipe Publishing

21ˢᵀ Century Coastal American Verses
By
Zack Dye

Zack Dye's powerful debut collection travels from sea to sea, shining a light on the ways our country's systems of oppression twist our sense of identity, freedom, love, and loss into an American mythos we wear like a hairshirt. Dye's unique experience as a white-presenting Mexican American, as a person who has climbed up and down the socio-economic ladder, and as someone who has lived and traveled across the country, produces a unique voice, sometimes pulling the reader in, sometimes shoving us away angrily, leaving us shaken.

"Zack Dye's poems channel Walt Whitman, if the American everyman had been writing more often from a place of blazing rage."
-Eliza Stricland, Senior Editor at *IEEE Spectrum*

"... fleeting moments of joy and knowledge in the midst of confusion, misunderstanding, frustration, anger, and self-deception, engendered by the false dichotomies of race, language, and otherness in America."
-Jean Harkin, author of *Night in Alcatraz: and Other Uncanny Tales*

Wherever Fine Books Are Sold

Also Available from Not a Pipe Publishing

INCANDESCENT
BY
AYODELE NZINGA

From the forward by K.M. Smith: *"Incandescent,* the brilliance of expression that Ayodele Nzinga has so lovingly crafted, is red hot in its urgency. It moves subtly, it shifts and crescendos and somersaults across time and space, through light and darkness, joy and pain. This fiery book of poetry comes at you quickly. Questions abound and answers permeate about justice and freedom and existence."

"I am overwhelmed by the pervasive African love expressed in this collection, but even more so by her profound recognition of Ancestor worship and their essential connection to our existence in the now and in the future. These poems, as she acknowledges, are not of her voice but of the ancestors speaking of our duty to them that we cannot escape. ... A continuation of her eternal moan and praise to ancestors, asking, pleading, praying. She is the new truth of the old truth. She is tribal history and eternity."
-Marvin X, author of *How to Recover from the Addiction to White Supremacy*, and *The Wisdom of Plato Negro: A Hustler's Guide to the Game Called Life*

Wherever Fine Books Are Sold

Also Available from Not a Pipe Publishing

Strongly Worded Women

The Best of the Year
of Publishing Women
An Anthology
Edited by
Sydney Culpepper

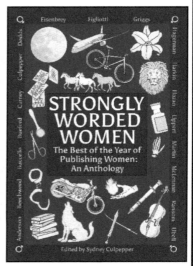

With stories by Maren Bradley Anderson,
Debby Dodds, Jean Harkin, Laura Hazan, Lori
Ubell, Chloe Hagerman, Lizzy Carney, Tonya
Lippert, Claudine Griggs, Taylor Buccello, Julia
Figliotti, Rosie Bueford, Elizabeth Beechwood,
LeeAnn Elwood McLennan, Heather S. Ransom,
Sydney Culpepper, and Karen Eisenbrey

Back in 2015, Not a Pipe Publishing announced
accepting author Kamila Shamsie's challenge
to the publishing industry to only publish
women authors in 2018. After publishing eight
novels by seven authors, they capped off their
Year of Publishing Women with an anthology
of 18 short stories by these amazing women
authors from across the country.

Wherever Fine Books Are Sold

Also Available from Not a Pipe Publishing

Shout

An Anthology of Resistance Poetry and Short Fiction

Edited by Benjamin Gorman and Zack Dye

With poems and short stories by **Rosanne Parry, Janet Burroway, Carolyn Adams, Benjamin Gorman, Lydia K. Valentine, Zack Dye, Rebecca Smolen, Eric Witchey, Heather S. Ransom, Joanna Michal Hoyt, Stephen Scott Whitaker, Karen Eisenbrey, Meagan Johanson, TJ Berg, Jennifer Lee Rossman, Carlton Herzog, Austin Case, Allan T. Price, K.A. Miltimore, Jill Hohnstein, Kurt Newton, Taliyah St. James, John Miller, Christopher Mark Rose**, and **Bethany Lee.**

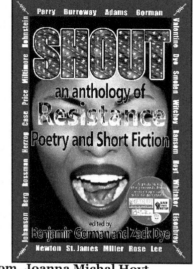

The 25 incredibly talented authors and poets in this anthology aren't politicians, policy wonks, or partisans. They're artists staring at the rising tide of fascism in the United States and asking you:
"What kind of world do you want to live in tomorrow?"
and "Who do you want to be today?"
And they aren't asking quietly.

Wherever Fine Books Are Sold

ALSO AVAILABLE FROM NOT A PIPE PUBLISHING

Don't Read This Book
by
Benjamin Gorman

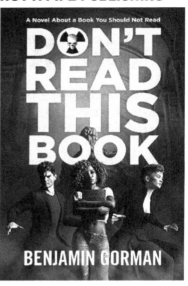

A Novel About a Book You Should Not Read

Magdalena Wallace is the greatest writer in the world. She just doesn't know it.

When she wakes up chained to a desk next to a stack of typed pages and the corpse of the person who read them, she learns just how dangerous her book can be. Rescued by a vampire, a werewolf, and a golem, she's on the run with the manuscript — and the fate of humanity — in her backpack, and a whole lot of monsters hot on her heels!

"…a whimsical, fast-paced, delight; snappily written, deliciously funny and smart, and full of affection for its characters."
- New York Times bestseller Chelsea Cain, author of *Heartsick*, *Mockingbird*, and *Gone*

"… smart, determined, and filled with really stunning prose … maybe one of the best books I've read!"
-Sydney Culpepper
author of *Pagetown*, editor of *Strongly Worded Women*

Wherever Fine Books Are Sold

ALSO AVAILABLE FROM NOT A PIPE PUBLISHING

When She

Leaves Me

a story told in poems
by

Benjamin Gorman

In his debut collection, Gorman relays the story of a shocking dissolution of two decades of marriage and his long crawl back to hope. Unflinching, unflattering, shocked and angry and selfish and ultimately generous, the poetry is aimed at readers open to empathy who can nourish their souls on a journey of healing.

"*When She Leaves Me* is a field of wildflowers that blooms after raging fires scorch the forest. These poems not only refuse to let sorrow and destruction have the final word, they are in fact only possible because they are born from that charred past life."
-Armin Tolentino, author of *We Meant to Bring It Home Alive*

"Gorman's voice bravely explores the pain that comes with the realization that ending what was meant to be a lifelong relationship at times is the best happily-ever-after one can hope for. I honestly couldn't put this work down."
-William V.S. Tubman III, author of *Anthem Mantra Light: Poetry/Inspiration*

Wherever Fine Books Are Sold

CPSIA information can be obtained
at www.ICGtesting.com
Printed in the USA
LVHW081659251021
701495LV00012B/459

9 781956 892017